preparing for marriage

God's plan for your life together

Preparing for Marriage: Study Guide

Published by
The Good Book Company Ltd
Elm House, 37 Elm Road
New Malden, Surrey KT3 3HB, UK
Tel: 0845 225 0880; Fax: 0845 225 0990
email: admin@thegoodbook.co.uk
website: www.thegoodbook.co.uk

The Good Book COMPANY

Unless indicated, all Scripture references are taken from the HOLY BIBLE, NEW INTERNATIONAL VERSION. Copyright © 1973, 1978, 1984 International Bible Society. Used by permission.

ISBN 13: 9781905564231

Printed in the UK

read this first!

Congratulations on your decision to get married!

By deciding to get married, you have chosen to do a brilliant thing, and we're delighted that you want to get married in church. By coming on this preparation course, we hope that you will gain some valuable insight into the true nature of marriage and how to build a happy, secure and healthy relationship, which will last through the years.

As we run through this course, we'll see God's 'take' on marriage—he's a big fan—but then he would be, because he invented it! God is concerned that your marriage is built on firm ground, and will become a relationship that lasts.

That's why, as well as covering a number of practical aspects of your relationship, we will also explore the ultimate model for marriage, namely, the self-giving and on-going love of the Lord Jesus Christ.

During each session you will:

★ Discuss one aspect of your relationship;

★ Read together some verses from the Bible;

★ Hear a short explanation of those verses;

★ Be invited to discuss what you have heard, and ask any questions you may have.

In addition, there are some things for you to think about at home, and some practical tips to consider. Hope you find them useful! It's well worth setting some time aside each week to work through the questions in preparation for the next session, and to talk through any issues that have been raised for you as a couple through the course. There will be plenty of time to talk through any ideas or problems you have at your next meeting.

There's a lot to learn about marriage—it's very different to any other relationship you may have had in the past—even different from the relationship you have with your fiancé/e. That is why it's worth doing some preparation. And as you do so, I hope you will discover some new and wonderful depths to your relationship, which will bring you closer together.

I also hope that you will discover how a new and wonderful relationship with the God who made you and loves you can be a part of your lives together—because God's plan for your marriage is bigger and more amazing than you ever dreamed it could be...

Pete Jackson

P.S. The course is designed to be led by a minister who will give you an explanation of the Christian view of marriage. You can listen to my version of these short talks online at www.thegoodbook.co.uk (search for Preparing for Marriage).

a marriage made in heaven?

1

Write down:

★ *What was it that first attracted you to your future wife/husband, and what attracts you to them now?*

_____

_____

_____

_____

★ *What do you think is best about them?*

_____

_____

_____

_____

★ *Why do you want to get married?*

_____

_____

_____

_____

---

how it all started

GOD THE CREATOR...

- of men and women
- of everything
- of marriage

MARRIAGE...

- ...for one man and one woman...
- ...for life

GOD...

- made everything and is therefore in charge
- can be known by us because he has spoken
- has even shown us what he is like in Jesus

Questions for discussion:

★ *What do you think of God's blueprint for marriage?*

_____

★ *Has anything you've heard today surprised you?*

_____

_____

★ *If God made everything (and everyone), how should people treat him?*

_____

_____

Genesis 1 v 26-28

26 Then God said, 'Let us make man in our image, in our likeness, and let them rule over the fish of the sea and the birds of the air, over the livestock, over all the earth, and over all the creatures that move along the ground.' 27 So God created man in his own image, in the image of God he created him; male and female he created them. 28 God blessed them and said to them, 'Be fruitful and increase in number; fill the earth and subdue it. Rule over the fish of the sea and the birds of the air and over every living creature that moves on the ground.'

Mark 10 v 6-9

6 At the beginning of creation God 'made them male and female.' 7 'For this reason a man will leave his father and mother and be united to his wife, 8 and the two will become one flesh.' So they are no longer two, but one. 9 Therefore what God has joined together, let man not separate.

Colossians 1 v 15-16

[Jesus] is the image of the invisible God ... For by him all things were created: things in heaven and on earth, visible and invisible ... all things were created by him and for him.

Mark 4 v 35-41

35 That day when evening came, he said to his disciples, 'Let us go over to the other side.' 36 Leaving the crowd behind, they took him along, just as he was, in the boat. There were also other boats with him. 37 A furious squall came up, and the waves broke over the boat, so that it was nearly swamped. 38 Jesus was in the stern, sleeping on a cushion. The disciples woke him and said to him, 'Teacher, don't you care if we drown?' 39 He got up, rebuked the wind and said to the waves, 'Quiet! Be still!' Then the wind died down and it was completely calm. 40 He said to his disciples, 'Why are you so afraid? Do you still have no faith?'
41 They were terrified and asked each other, 'Who is this? Even the wind and the waves obey him!'

to think about together...

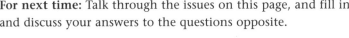

1 *Marriage is the closest relationship between two human beings—they become 'one flesh'. How will this affect or change your relationship with:*

- *any children you may have?*

- *your parents or parents-in-law?*

- *brothers, sisters, best mates?*

2 *What boundaries will you need to set for these other relationships?*

3 *How will you make sure that you grow closer together as a couple, rather than get stale or drift apart?*

Here are some ideas that others have found helpful:

★ Spend half an hour every day talking together—each ask the other about their day, worries, hopes, plans, frustrations, etc.

★ Plan to spend two uninterrupted hours alone every week—just enjoying one another—having fun together!

★ Every few months or so, plan a day away by yourselves.

★ Find an activity that you can do together.

★ Plan to eat together

★ If you have children, try to have two or three days away together on your own once a year.

Discuss with your partner how you can put these ideas into practice.

For next time: Talk through the issues on this page, and fill in and discuss your answers to the questions opposite.

the problem with marriage

Write down:

★ *What do you think will be difficult in marriage?*

_____

_____

_____

★ *What is it about you that will make being married to you difficult?*

_____

_____

_____

★ *What is it about your partner that will make being married to them difficult?*

_____

_____

_____

★ *Why do you think these things might be a problem?*

_____

_____

_____

the heart of the problem

ALL PEOPLE...

- Think they know better than God, and so ignore Him while living in His world.

- Think they are in charge and so put themselves first.

- Think they are okay with God,
  but are actually guilty of rebelling against Him.

SO WHAT?

- Our world and lives are messed up.

- We are in a broken relationship with God.

- God will judge and make sure justice is done.

- God will punish all who are guilty.

- The punishment is being cut off from God forever ('hell').

Questions for discussion:

★ *What did you think God thought of you before today (or what did you think about yourself)?*

_____

★ *Has anything you've heard today surprised you?*

_____

_____

★ *Do you agree or disagree that you are a rebel in God's world?*

_____

_____

Genesis 2 v 16-17

[16] And the LORD God commanded the man, 'You are free to eat from any tree in the garden; [17] but you must not eat from the tree of the knowledge of good and evil, for when you eat of it you will surely die.'

Genesis 3 v 1-6

[1] Now the serpent was more crafty than any of the wild animals the LORD God had made. He said to the woman, 'Did God really say, "You must not eat from any tree in the garden"?' [2] The woman said to the serpent, 'We may eat fruit from the trees in the garden, [3] but God did say, "You must not eat fruit from the tree that is in the middle of the garden, and you must not touch it, or you will die."'
[4] 'You will not surely die,' the serpent said to the woman. [5] 'For God knows that when you eat of it your eyes will be opened, and you will be like God, knowing good and evil.'

[6] When the woman saw that the fruit of the tree was good for food and pleasing to the eye, and also desirable for gaining wisdom, she took some and ate it. She also gave some to her husband, who was with her, and he ate it.

Romans 3 v 10-12

[10] As it is written: 'There is no-one righteous, not even one; [11] there is no one who understands, no one who seeks God. [12] All have turned away, they have together become worthless; there is no one who does good, not even one.'

Hebrews 9 v 27

Man is destined to die once, and after that to face judgement.

to think about together...

The main problem with marriage is that we are all sinful (self-centred, rebels against God)—and this directly affects all our relationships.

In marriage, our freedom to be self-centred is seriously restricted. We are no longer able to do just what *we* want, but must consider the needs and desires of our partner. Conflict is almost inevitable!

1. *What are the things most likely to cause conflict between you?*

2. *How, as a couple, do you resolve conflict at the moment?*

3. *How do you think you could improve conflict resolution?*

4. *When is the best time to resolve difficulties?*

5. *What are you like at backing down and saying sorry?*
   What are you like at accepting an apology and forgiving?

Discuss the merits of the following 4 ways of dealing with conflict:
- ★ **Going on the attack** (forcing my opinion on my partner)
- ★ **Passively submitting** (just agreeing to keep the peace)
- ★ **Cutting a deal** (each give and take a little)
- ★ **Negotiation** (what is best for you both as a couple).

The biggest areas of conflict in marriage are:
- ★ **Money**—how it is organised and spent
- ★ **Children**—how many, when, and sharing the care workload
- ★ **The wider family**—how much and how often will you see them?

If you haven't done so already, you need to talk through each of these areas and be sure that you understand any different attitudes you may have.

Discuss with your partner how you can put these ideas into practice.

the sacrifice of marriage 3

Write down:

★ *What personal qualities will you bring to this marriage?*

- _____
- _____
- _____

★ *What sort of husband / wife do you think you will be?*

_____

_____

_____

_____

★ *What are your expectations for your husband/wife? (What do you want from them?)*

_____

_____

_____

_____

_____

---

the model for marriage

LOVING SACRIFICE

- Jesus was selfless—even to death

- Jesus took the 'rap' for the way we have treated God (Jesus was punished for our sin in our place).

- Jesus was cut off from God so we don't have to be.

SO WHAT?

- God must love you very much to let his Son die for you.

- Jesus' death opens the way for us to come back to God and be forgiven by him—and not get what we deserve for ignoring him (for being 'sinful').

- We can't 'sit on the fence' regarding Jesus.

Questions for discussion:

★ *Did you realise how much God loves you?*
What is remarkable about the love he shows us at the cross?

_____

_____

★ *Why do you think Peter emphasises that Jesus was 'righteous' (never did anything wrong)?*

_____

_____

_____

Ephesians 5 v 25

²² Wives, submit to your husbands as to the Lord. ²³ For the husband is the head of the wife as Christ is the head of the church, his body, of which he is the Saviour. ²⁴ Now as the church submits to Christ, so also wives should submit to their husbands in everything. ²⁵ Husbands, love your wives, just as Christ loved the church and gave himself up for her.'

Mark 15 v 22-25, 33-34

²²They brought Jesus to the place called Golgotha (which means The Place of the Skull). ²³Then they offered him wine mixed with myrrh, but he did not take it. ²⁴And they crucified him. Dividing up his clothes, they cast lots to see what each would get. ²⁵It was the third hour when they crucified him.

³³At the sixth hour darkness came over the whole land until the ninth hour. ³⁴ And at the ninth hour Jesus cried out in a loud voice, *'Eloi, Eloi, lama sabachthani?'*—which means, 'My God, my God, why have you forsaken me?'

1Peter 3 v 18

Christ died for sins once for all, the righteous for the unrighteous, to bring you to God.

to think about together...

1. What do you think makes your future spouse feel loved?

2. How will you sacrificially serve each other?
   What will your love for each other mean that you have to give up?

3. What habits or behaviour in yourself should you seek to change for the sake of your spouse and marriage?

4. Sex is the ultimate expression of giving of self to your spouse. How might sex become selfish? How will you aim to avoid this?

TOP TIPS

★ Tell each other what you respond to most... words (compliments, thanks, encouragement), actions, surprises, gifts, touch, time together or something else.

★ Don't make assumptions about the jobs that you do around the house—cleaning, cooking, laundry, DIY, gardening and accounts. Work out how these tasks will be done together, and *express your gratitude to each other* for doing them.

★ Recognise that change can be extremely hard! Some of our bad habits and attitudes are deeply ingrained, and your partner will need encouragement to keep working at it.

★ Don't keep affection just for the bedroom! Loving talk, touching, listening, holding hands and all that stuff should be a normal part of your married life together. It builds trust and closeness.

the Promises

Write down what you think about the marriage 'deal':

- Your 'vows' are of the utmost seriousness (as the wedding service puts it, they are 'solemn'). You will make them to each other before God.

  _____

  _____

- You will publicly declare your willingness to enter into marriage with each other, before your families and friends.

  _____

  _____

- Your commitment is unconditional: *'For better, for worse; for richer, for poorer; in sickness and in health ...'*

  _____

  _____

- You will say *'I will'*, not *'I do'*! Your commitment is for life: *'... to love and to cherish, until death us do part'.*

  _____

  _____

**If this isn't for you, don't be afraid to pull out of this deal
BEFORE you make the commitment.**

the promise of God

John 3 v 36
Whoever believes in the Son has eternal life,
but whoever rejects the Son will not see life,
for God's wrath remains on him.

OPTION 1: REJECT JESUS

- Continue to live life my own way (with me in charge).

- Continue to ignore God and what he has done for us in the person of Jesus.

- Continue to think that I know better than God.

- Remain unforgiven and facing God's right anger at my sin.

- Cut off from God... forever

OPTION 2: BELIEVE IN JESUS

- Trust Jesus as your Saviour, knowing that He has paid the penalty for your sin.

- Receive eternal life and forgiveness as a free gift—and so be in a right relationship with God.

- Live with Jesus as the boss of your life ('Lord').

THE FORK IN THE ROAD

- Which way are you going?

Questions for discussion:

★ *What's your reaction to what you are required to promise to each other?*

_____

_____

★ *Is there anything that you're not sure about?*

_____

★ *What's your reaction to the promise of God?*

_____

★ *Is there anything stopping you from believing in Jesus?*

_____

A prayer for when you are ready:

Dear God,

I know I don't deserve to be accepted by you.

I am guilty of ignoring you and I need forgiveness.

Thank you that Jesus died for me so that I can be forgiven.

Thank you that he rose from the dead to give me new life.

Please come into my life—forgive me and change me.

And help me to live with Jesus as my Lord and Saviour.

Amen.

to think about together...

The promises you will make on your wedding day are life-long: '...for better for worse, for richer for poorer, in sickness and in health, till death us do part...'

1. *How will you deal with the situation when you find yourself attracted to someone else?*

2. *There may be times, sometimes prolonged, when sickness, or simply the tiredness that comes with work or young children, will mean that sex is off the agenda. How will you cope with that in a way that draws you together, rather than pushes you apart?*

TOP TIPS

★ **Outside attractions**

Be honest! Share inappropriate feelings of attraction with someone else (preferably your spouse, but if not, then a trusted friend of the same sex). This will often help the feelings to die down.

★ **Money**

Joint accounts or separate? There is no right or wrong way to organise your finances: do a mini-survey of some married friends (or your parents) to find out how they organise things—and the advantages and disadvantages of their approach. Decide what will work for you.

★ **Debt**

Money is often a major source of problems in marriage. If you are in debt, do talk together and get good advice about how you can get out of it. Problems only get worse if you remain silent.

SEX
One Flesh *Greg and Amelia Clarke (Matthias Media)*
This friendly, enjoyable and highly informative introduction to sex in marriage explains the Bible's teaching on sex, the practicalities of beginning a sexual relationship, and the kinds of problems which commonly emerge for couples. It also considers the consequences of sexual sin for a married couple.

MARRIAGE
God, Sex and Marriage *John Richardson (The Good Book Company)*
A short introduction to the big issues from the pages of New Testament.

The Diamond Marriage *Simon Vibert (Christian Focus Publications)*
How can joy in marriage be revived? his Biblical perspective on marriage is packed with insight, wisdom and wit.

Don't they make a lovely couple? *John and Anne Benton (CFP)*
Six important questions for couples to work through.

UNDERSTANDING THE CHRISTIAN FAITH
The Bible!
No better place to start than by reading one of the gospels—we recommend Luke—and to start thinking about who Jesus is, and what he has done. Find a modern translation like the NIV, and read it in small sections, writing down your questions and observations to discuss with your partner, or with an established Christian.

A Fresh Start *John Chapman (The Good Book Company)*
An honest and down-to-earth read about: just what God has done for us through his son, Jesus; how we can know it is true; what the alternatives are; and what we should do about it.

Christianity Explored *Rico Tice (The Good Book Company)*
Drawing from the book of Mark in the Bible the book explores who Jesus was, what his aims were, and what it means to follow him. Concise, entertaining and honest, it's an ideal book for anyone with little or no experience of Christianity.

These titles are available from your local Christian bookshop, or visit www.thegoodbook.co.uk

evaluation form

Please tick the appropriate answers. Please feel free not to answer all or even any of the questions. Do be honest and frank.

Name _____

1. *How would you say this course has made you think differently as you have prepared for your marriage?*

   _____

   _____

2. *Which aspect have you most enjoyed?*

   _____

3. *Which part have you least enjoyed?*

   _____

   _____

4. *Are there any areas that were not touched upon that you would have found helpful?*

   _____

   _____

5. *Before you began this course, how would you have described yourself?*
   - ☐ I didn't believe in God
   - ☐ I wasn't sure if God existed or not
   - ☐ I believed in God but not in Jesus
   - ☐ A Christian (personally committed to Jesus)
   - ☐ Something else _____

6. *Where would you say you stand now in relation to Jesus?*

☐ I have genuinely repented and come to believe in Jesus as my Lord and Saviour

☐ I am interested in learning more but, as yet, not ready to believe in Jesus as Lord and Saviour.

☐ Other _____

7. *If you have not believed in Jesus as your personal Saviour, what do you think is stopping you?*

_____

_____

8. *Are there any questions for which you would still like an answer?*

_____

_____

_____

_____

_____

_____

10. *Would you like to join a course that explores the meaning of the Christian faith in greater depth?*

☐ Yes

☐ No

Please return this form to the person who did the course with you.